pulp FASHION

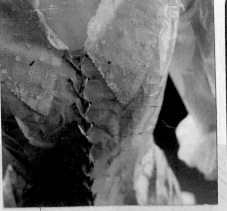

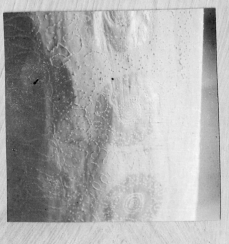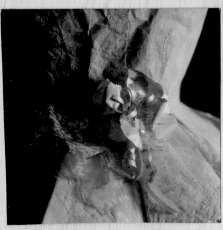

pulp
FASHION
the art of Isabelle de Borchgrave

Jill D'Alessandro

Fine Arts Museums of San Francisco
DelMonico Books • Prestel
MUNICH BERLIN LONDON NEW YORK

Contents

John E. Buchanan, Jr.

Director's Foreword

I still recall the moment I first learned of the work of Isabelle de Borchgrave.
Some friends were in Venice and made a pilgrimage to the Museo Fortuny,
the opulent palazzo dedicated to the life and work of the master of pleated
fashions. The museum was then presenting an exhibition called *Un mondo
di carta* (*A World of Paper*), a spectacular and utterly engrossing installation
of paper costumes by de Borchgrave. Upon hearing about it, I planned a
trip to Brussels to visit her magical studio, where I couldn't help but marvel
at the singularity and scope of her oeuvre. We began immediately to plan
Pulp Fashion: The Art of Isabelle de Borchgrave. I am proud to say that this
exhibition, so appropriately presented in the galleries of our Legion of
Honor museum, is the first to offer an overview of the artist's most important bodies of work: from the white dresses and *Papiers à la Mode* to the
Fortuny and Medici collections and her newest creations.

The Legion of Honor—home of the Fine Arts Museums' collection of
European decorative arts and painting—is a treasure trove of potential
sources for an artist like de Borchgrave. Indeed, her enthusiasm for the
paintings she discovered there inspired the commission of a group of
original paper costumes under the auspices of our Collection Connections
program. Generously funded by The Annenberg Foundation, Collection
Connections aims to present new works that reinterpret traditional
objects from the Museums' permanent collection. For each project,
artist and curator draw inspiration from the permanent collection,
offering nontraditional connections that provide visual and educational

Eleanora of Toledo, 2006
Inspired by a ca. 1545 portrait of Eleanora
and her son Giovanni de' Medici by Agnolo
Bronzino in the collection of the Galleria
degli Uffizi, Florence

opportunities to explain, interpret, and recontextualize the objects on display. For the Collection Connections segment of *Pulp Fashion*, de Borchgrave has chosen to respond to paintings by Konstantin Makovsky, Massimo Stanzione, Anthony van Dyck, and Jacob-Ferdinand Voet. We are delighted to be able to feature the first of the Collection Connections commissions produced by de Borchgrave, based on Stanzione's striking portrait of a Neapolitan woman, in this publication, which is supported in part by a grant from the Friends of Fiber Art International. We are also exceedingly grateful to Lonna Wais for her sponsorship of the exhibition. Additional support is provided by Elizabeth W. Vobach.

A project of this complexity, involving international collaboration and such intricate and delicate art objects, could not have been possible without the expertise of our talented Fine Arts Museums staff. Curator Jill D'Alessandro has guided the exhibition and catalogue with creativity and flair, bringing her deep knowledge of textiles and fashion to bear on the presentation of these remarkable paper costumes. To complement the artist's work, Jill has made a selection of key Western tapestries and textiles from the Museums' extensive permanent collection, greatly enriching our presentation of de Borchgrave's oeuvre. Lynn Federle Orr, the Fine Arts Museums' curator in charge of European art, generously shared her knowledge of our paintings collection, helping the artist refine her choices for the newly commissioned works. Karen Levine skillfully edited the manuscript for this volume and managed every detail of its publication. Bill White and his team designed a visually stunning exhibition experience, enhanced by Bill Huggins's masterful lighting design. Krista Brugnara capably coordinated the exhibition logistics. Debra Evans, Sarah Gates, and Beth Szuhay lent their many skills to the installation; the Registration Department oversaw the transfer of the collection with typical care; and the Marketing and Graphic Design team also made significant contributions to the project. Department of Textile Arts intern Marlena Cannon provided invaluable assistance during the development of the exhibition and catalogue. Thanks also to the department's office manager, Trish Daly. Outside the Museums, Marquand Books, Mary DelMonico, and Prestel deserve gratitude for their enthusiastic partnership on the publication.

Having visited de Borchgrave's studio, I know that she relies on an outstanding team of collaborators to help bring her work to fruition. First and foremost, we are grateful to her husband, Werner de Borchgrave, for serving as a vital lifeline to Brussels, managing everything with such precision that the artist is left free to create. The Fine Arts Museums join the de Borchgraves in thanking everyone associated with Créations Isabelle de Borchgrave, particularly exhibition manager Laetitia d'Ursel; project manager Priscilla Bracht; stylists Rita Brown, Mathie Claeys, Anna Ervamaa, Cécile de Jaegher, Audrey Jacques, Zuzana Krizova, and Audrey Lienart; assistants Ludovic Ledent, Céline Libert, Dora Michel, Julie Sneiders, and Thais Vanderheyden; videographer Nicolas de Borchgrave; designer/photographer Pauline de Borchgrave; and photographers Andreas von Einsiedel, Jean-Pierre Gabriel, Philippe Leclercq, and René Stoeltie. The creation of the Medici collection was made possible through the sponsorship of Eric Freymond, Nicolas Puech-Hermès, Christiane Martroye de Joly, Sybille de Spoelberch, and Faïencerie de Gien.

These acknowledgments would not be complete without a final note of gratitude to the excessively talented Isabelle de Borchgrave. Thank you for letting us dream.

Jill D'Alessandro

fashioning HISTORY

I am on the edge. It is as if I am riding in a glass carriage. ISABELLE DE BORCHGRAVE

For more than fifteen years, the Belgian artist Isabelle de Borchgrave has been producing a completely original body of work that is quite easy to explain but very difficult to categorize. Her central project has been to re-create exquisite, life-size historical costumes entirely from paper. From afar, de Borchgrave's creations appear to be masterpieces of trompe l'oeil. Taking inspiration from the rich depictions in early European paintings, iconic costumes in museum collections, photographs, sketches, and even literary descriptions, de Borchgrave skillfully works paper to achieve the effect of textiles: crumpling, pleating, braiding, feathering, and painting the surface. The culmination of a long and restless artistic career, de Borchgrave's mature work is best understood not only by examining her artistic processes, her sources, and the theoretical discourse that surrounds painting and costume, but also by considering the artist's own social and creative context.

Formally trained in painting and drawing at the Centre des Arts Décoratifs and the Royal Academy of Fine Arts in Brussels, de Borchgrave began her artistic career designing dresses of hand-painted fabric for special occasions; though they were initially intended only for herself and friends, she quickly developed a client list. It was the late 1960s, and the works reflected the optimistic spirit of the youthquake. De Borchgrave strove to make a

The artist at work on a piece based on Massimo Stanzione's *Woman in Neapolitan Costume*, 2010

statement with her ensembles, painting each dress with scenes inspired by the Ballets Russes, bazaars, and her own travels to the Indies and Turkey. However, her practice soon took a more pragmatic direction: she spent the following decades designing textile and furnishing lines, including table linens, printed fabrics, ceramics, and stationery.[1]

A fateful encounter in 1994 marked a turning point. In New York to attend the Metropolitan Opera premiere of *La Traviata*, with sets and costumes designed by fellow Belgian Thierry Bosquet, de Borchgrave met the Canadian costume historian, conservator, and theatrical designer Rita Brown. The next day, together they toured the galleries of the Costume Institute at the Metropolitan Museum of Art, an experience that rekindled de Borchgrave's love of fashion. Brown was working with the preeminent historical costume collector Martin Kamer, and she later brought de Borchgrave with her when she examined his collection. There, de Borchgrave was able to handle museum-quality dresses from the eighteenth and nineteenth centuries—an opportunity enjoyed by few individuals. Brown and de Borchgrave spent days turning the costumes inside out, examining the fabrics, seams, and construction. "Those dresses had such a capacity to amaze," reflects de Borchgrave. "They were so beautiful that they became a powerful source of inspiration. They gave me the desire to create."[2]

18]

Brown soon became what she called de Borchgrave's "willing accomplice"[3] in the creation of the first thirty paper costumes, a series they came to title *Papiers à la Mode*. Over the next four years (1994–1998), Brown traveled to Brussels for five- to six-week periods of intense collaboration. They combed museum collections and books on fashion to find sources of inspiration. They learned by trial and error, as Brown, trained in historical costume construction, soon realized that rules for working with textiles did not apply to paper.

De Borchgrave, meanwhile, was experimenting with different media to create elaborate trompe l'oeil surfaces for each costume. For an American day suit (pages 40–41), she varnished the back of the paper to give it depth and tone, used a comb to imitate silk moiré, and mixed iridescent water-color with acrylic to suggest the sheen of an overshot weave.[4] De Borchgrave discovered that the simpler the fabric, the more difficult it was to duplicate. And even more than the actual dress, it was the fabric that captivated her. She selected historical pieces precisely for their distinctive textiles. For

LEFT Isabelle de Borchgrave. Margaret Layton evening jacket (detail), 2001. Inspired by a ca. 1610 jacket and a portrait by Marcus Geeraerts the younger in the collection of the Victoria and Albert Museum, London. 20⅛ × 17⅜ × 10¼ in. (51 × 44 × 26 cm). Collection of the artist.

RIGHT Jacobean embroidered forehead cloth, England, ca. 1600–1625. 15½ × 7¼ in. (36.8 × 18.4 cm). Fine Arts Museums of San Francisco, 1995.24.

example, she re-created Margaret Layton's jacket, the best-documented example of English Jacobean embroidery—a style that flourished in the early seventeenth century, during the reign of King James I (see above). Both the jacket and a portrait of Layton wearing it are in the collection of London's Victoria and Albert Museum, and they serve as touchstones for textile and costume scholars alike. De Borchgrave explains, "I think it was the love of fabric that encouraged me to create these dresses, to bring them back to life through the purity and simplicity of paper."[5]

In 1998 de Borchgrave and Brown mounted their first exhibition, *Papiers à la Mode*, at the Musée de l'Impression sur Étoffes in Mulhouse, France. The overwhelming success of this exhibition generated a world tour, and the paper fashions traveled from the United Kingdom to the United States and on to Japan, Turkey, and Brazil. Meanwhile, de Borchgrave's work continued to evolve. Whereas *Papiers à la Mode* focused on the history of costume, her subsequent series have become increasingly cinematic, displayed in immersive environments that verge on installation art.

Her studio has also evolved. In the spirit of Andy Warhol's Factory, de Borchgrave's Brussels atelier today teems with young designers, many of them recent graduates of art schools in Brussels, Antwerp, and Ghent. De Borchgrave clearly thrives on this dynamic atmosphere of collaboration; her work has become more elaborate and adventurous, as seen in series based on the eccentric designs of Mariano Fortuny y Madrazo (pages 48–61), the luxurious court dress of the Medici dynasty of

Isabelle de Borchgrave and studio collaborators at work on a piece
inspired by Agnolo Bronzino's portrait of Eleanora of Toledo, 2006

Renaissance Italy (pages 64–81), and paintings in the collection of the Fine Arts Museums of San Francisco (pages 84–93). As in a true fashion atelier, each artist/designer, under de Borchgrave's direction, specializes in a particular aspect of a costume's creation: building the armature, constructing the dress pattern, painting the solid-color ground of the "fabric," crafting individual pearls and ribbons, or cutting delicate paper feathers (see left and pages 86–89). All of these processes are shared among the team; however, when it comes to designing the trompe l'oeil surfaces of the paper, it is purely de Borchgrave's hand.

21]

Despite first appearances, these creations are not stringent copies of the originals; they are more like impressions. Throughout her career, de Borchgrave has worked in a variety of media—including paint, textiles, ceramics, and, ultimately, paper—and she continues to move between these disciplines. But it is de Borchgrave the painter who is perhaps the most forceful presence. When painting she works quickly and intuitively, though the detailing of each costume is painstakingly methodical. Her work thus oscillates between a free painterly style and a nearly fanatic compulsiveness. This inherent paradox is best exemplified in her remarkable handling of the lace collar and cuffs of Marie de' Medici's court dress (below and pages 80–81). De Borchgrave began by painting the intricate network of patterns in a fluid hand. She then carefully used a scalpel to cut out the negative spaces, leaving behind a beautiful, diaphanous web.

Isabelle de Borchgrave. Marie de' Medici (lace study), 2006. Inspired by a 1595 portrait by Pietro Facchetti in the collection of the Palazzo Lancellotti, Rome. 8¹¹/₁₆ × 28⅜ in. (22 × 72 cm), Collection of the artist.

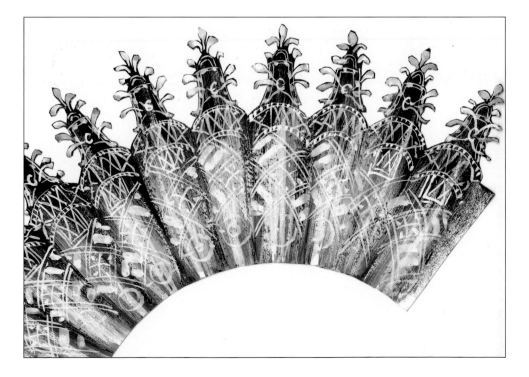

Jean-Auguste-Dominique Ingres. *Madame Moitessier*, 1856. 47¼ × 36¼ in. (120 × 92.1 cm). National Gallery, London, NG4821.

Tellingly, de Borchgrave's sources are often not actual costumes but painted portraits in which the subjects' iconic garments seem to take on their own identities. As costume scholar Aileen Ribeiro has argued, "A portrait suggests a precise moment in history, and often the costume is so important to the image that it transfixes the sitter in a kind of time-warp."[6] Many of de Borchgrave's elaborate court dresses found their muses in the paintings of the late eighteenth and early nineteenth centuries, the "portrait-painting age." Society painters of the time strove to find the correct balance between creating suitable likenesses of their sitters, including their subjects' elegant regalia, and allowing their own distinctive styles to flourish. Writing in the nineteenth century, the French poet and critic Charles Baudelaire astutely described a successful portrait as a dramatized biography; the artist must be an actor, "whose duty is to adopt any character and any costume."[7] De Borchgrave echoes this notion when she explains that while studying a work, she imagines the mindset of the artist who depicted the costume and tries to conjure the psyche of the subject.

Employing a thorough knowledge of both portrait painting and the history of costume, de Borchgrave enjoys playing with nuances. In one example, she coyly attributes a dress based on Jean-Auguste-Dominique Ingres's 1856 portrait of Marie-Clotilde-Inès Moitessier (left) to another woman: Empress Eugénie, the beautiful wife of Napoléon III who set the standards for fashion in the French court (page 35). Madame Moitessier posed in a gown of the finest Lyon silk—of the same sumptuous quality worn by Empress Eugénie, by request of her husband, to stimulate the Lyon textile industry. At a time when inside jokes have become epidemic in contemporary art, de Borchgrave satirizes the fads of generations past.

But in this act of recontextualization, with whom does de Borchgrave identify? Is it the woman who posed for the portrait, the master painter, or the "painter tailor"? Before the nineteenth century, fashionable artists often hired drapery painters to finish rendering costumes after the sittings were completed. Excelling in the painting of silks, satins, velvets, and embroideries, the best such artists commanded considerable fees and often had great influence on the composition of paintings and the choice of costumes. De Borchgrave's practice resuscitates the role of the painter tailor, extending the art of drapery into the realms of fashion, sculpture, and installation.

And yet, though de Borchgrave declares that her work seeks to express the timeless beauty of the past, her art remains quintessentially postmodern. De Borchgrave's career began in the late 1960s, coinciding with the American craze for paper dresses. Between 1967 and 1968, these whimsical paper gowns, many of them designed by leading artists or for marketing campaigns, took the fashion world by storm. Cheap, fun, and definitively pop, meant to be worn once or twice and discarded, they captured the zeitgeist of 1960s. Harry Gordon sold his "poster dresses" (below) for three dollars apiece; other fashion designers, such as Elisa Daggs, Bonnie Cashin, Rudi Gernreich, Bill Blass, and Pierre Cardin, sold paper dresses for sums that ranged from ten to two hundred dollars.[8]

23]

Installation view of Joyce Kozloff's
An Interior Decorated (1978–1979) at
Tibor de Nagy Gallery, New York, 1979.

Some critics have asserted that de Borchgrave's finely crafted works of art
are the very antithesis of the 1960s paper shifts,[9] but the artist came to the
medium of paper for similar reasons. The paper dresses were made to be
accessible to everyone; there was a freedom in being able to purchase a
statement piece for pocket change. In much the same way, the inexpensive,
ephemeral material of paper gave de Borchgrave complete artistic freedom—
and it is the transient quality of her medium that most captivates the viewer.
Unlike expensive luxury fabrics, de Borchgrave's creations feel inclusive—
they do not carry with them the stigma of wealth and class. The work
invites us in and encourages us to participate in the pageant of history. As
de Borchgrave points out, it is "the history and perhaps more, the legend—
that renders it more accessible, more alive."[10]

Inclusiveness, decoration, exoticism, and craftsmanship are likewise
hallmarks of the Pattern and Decoration movement, which emerged in the
United States in the mid-1970s, during de Borchgrave's own formative years
as an artist. Pattern and Decoration, considered the first postmodern art
movement, is closely associated with the work of artists such as Jane A.
Kaufman, Joyce Kozloff, Robert Kushner, Miriam Schapiro, and Ned Smyth.

Reacting against the coldness of Minimalism, they reintroduced a decorative art based on ornamentation and vibrant colors. Embracing the pluralist ethos of postmodernism, these artists drew from a broad array of source material. Like de Borchgrave, they were passionate about patterning, non-Western culture, and travel. They looked to the exotic past of Asia and the Middle East and were influenced by Islamic art. They created large, boldly colored paintings and filled their canvases with luxuriant patterns.

Many of these artists eventually ventured into installation work that combined painting, sculpture, architecture, and the applied arts, producing environments intended to envelop the viewer in beauty (see left). In 1979 Smyth, describing the motivations of the Pattern and Decoration artists, wrote, "Decoration represents a move . . . towards humanism. I want to seduce, excite and move people by amassing decorative, physical, historical and archetypal images and objects."[11] Working on another continent a full decade later, with no personal connection to these artists, de Borchgrave independently arrived at a practice that shares much with the goals of her American counterparts. It is as if she had answered Kozloff's call for "an art of affirmation: additive, personal, decorative, lyrical, rococo, eclectic, exotic, complex, ornamented, and warm."[12]

As is clear from the work of de Borchgrave, along with artists such as Polly Apfelbaum, Andrea Higgins, and Yinka Shonibare, the legacy of Pattern and Decoration has been considerable.[13] But de Borchgrave's voice is unique. Unlike the exponents of Pattern and Decoration, she is not reacting against a predominant art movement, and unlike her younger contemporaries, she is not making a political statement. There is no evident subversion in this work; in fact, her oeuvre presents an innocent allure that is unusual in our times. Despite a rapidly changing world, de Borchgrave strives to "keep in my hands . . . the best of the past."[14]

NOTES

1. De Borchgrave continues to design a number of products for the retail market. Among her various projects, she is currently working with the company Caspari to create specialty paper products for museum gift shops.

2. Barbara and René Stoeltie, *Paper Illusions: The Art of Isabelle de Borchgrave* (New York: Harry N. Abrams, 2008), n.p.

3. June Ducas, "A Tissue a Fichu All Ball Gown," *The World of Interiors* 19, no. 1 (January 1999): 105.

4. Ibid.

5. Stoeltie, *Paper Illusions*, n.p.

6. Aileen Ribeiro, *The Art of Dress: Fashion in England and France, 1750–1820* (New Haven, CT: Yale University Press, 1995), 6.

7. Charles Baudelaire, *Art in Paris, 1845–1862: Salons and Other Exhibitions Reviewed by Charles Baudelaire*, trans. and ed. J. Mayne (London: Phaidon, 1965), 190.

8. See Vassilis Zidianakis, *Rrripp!! Paper Fashion* (Athens: ATOPOS Foundation, 2007).

9. Anne-Marie Schiro, "Patterns," *New York Times*, June 22, 1999.

10. Stoeltie, *Paper Illusions*, n.p.

11. Irving Sandler, *Art of the Postmodern Era: From the Late 1960s to the Early 1990s* (Boulder, CO: Westview Press, 1998), 151.

12. Joyce Kozloff, artist statement for the exhibition *Ten Approaches to the Decorative* (Alessandra Gallery, New York, 1976), quoted in Sandler, *Art of the Postmodern Era*, 151.

13. See *Pattern and Decoration: An Ideal Vision in American Art, 1975–1985*, ed. Anne Swartz (New York: Hudson River Museum, 2007).

14. Catherine Calvert, "Artistry à la Mode," *Victoria* 13, no. 6 (June 1999).

De Borchgrave's exploration of paper fashions began in 1994 with *Papiers à la Mode*, a series that re-creates iconic looks from key periods in fashion history. Largely inspired by the Kyoto Costume Institute publication *Revolution in Fashion: European Clothing, 1715–1815*, the series pays special attention to the critical period spanning the eighteenth and beginning of the nineteenth centuries—a time of dramatic evolution in the dress of the European courts. From a contemporary perspective, the dresses in the collection may seem equally extravagant; however, close study of the works reveals details that costume historians recognize as signifiers of social change, from the choice of fabric to the tightness of a bodice or the fullness of a skirt.

Like any historian, de Borchgrave understands that the accurate presentation of these looks is not a matter of simply reconstructing the silhouette and accessorizing the mannequin. "Although my inspiration springs from period dresses in museum collections and books, they are all subject to my poetic license," she explains. The pieces "are just a wink at history." De Borchgrave astutely selected costumes worn by legendary historical figures whose very names conjure visions of ideal beauty, opulent dress, and extravagant court life. It is no coincidence that the work focuses on the Rococo style of the eighteenth century, a time of economic prosperity when certain women attained social prominence as fashion style makers. Notable among them are the influential Madame de Pompadour (1721–1764), who defined the Rococo aesthetic, and Marie-Antoinette (1755–1793), who, despite her well-documented extravagances, was largely responsible for the transition from Rococo to Neoclassicism in costume.

Interestingly, *Papiers à la Mode* does not fail to document a subsequent paradigm shift in fashion. With the rise of the couturiers in the late nineteenth century—starting with Charles Frederick Worth (1825–1895)—it was suddenly the designers, not the wearers, who were surrounded by mystique. Their names became the very identifiers of style.

papiers À LA MODE

Elizabeth I court dress, 2001

Inspired by a ca. 1599 portrait by the studio of Nicholas Hilliard at
Hardwick Hall, Derbyshire

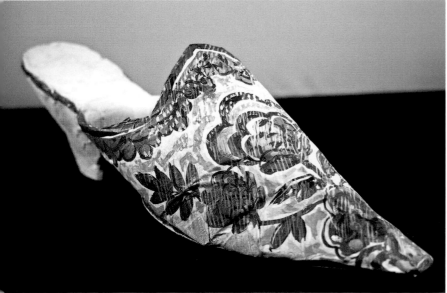

Madame de Pompadour court dress and shoe, 2001
Inspired by a ca. 1755 portrait by Maurice-Quentin
de la Tour in the collection of the Musée du Louvre,
Paris, and shoes in the collection of the Costume Institute,
the Metropolitan Museum of Art, New York

Marie-Antoinette gown, 2001

Inspired by a ca. 1776 engraving in the collection
of the Musée du Louvre, Paris

Empress Eugénie evening dress, 2001

Inspired by the 1856 painting *Madame Moitessier*
by Jean-Auguste-Dominique Ingres in the
collection of the National Gallery, London

34]

Worth evening gown and shoe, 1994

Based on an 1898 dress designed by Charles Frederick Worth in the collection of the
Costume Institute, the Metropolitan Museum of Art, New York

English sporting dress, 1998

Based on a ca. 1870 ensemble in the collection of the Victoria and Albert Museum, London

American day suit and hat, 1998
Based on a ca. 1900 ensemble in the
collection of the Museum at FIT,
New York

Paul Poiret evening ensemble, 1997

Inspired by ca. 1912 ensembles designed by
Paul Poiret in the collections of the Costume Institute,
the Metropolitan Museum of Art, New York; and the
Museum of the City of New York

PAUL POIRET
a Paris

Collection Metropolitan Museum

Poiret 1912
Satin lamp shade Dress
Silk Satin a Beaded Flowers
embroider

Evening dress, 2000
Based on a ca. 1924 dress designed by Coco Chanel in the collection of
the Victoria and Albert Museum, London

Invited by Venice's Museo Fortuny to create a body of work inspired by the Spanish-born master, de Borchgrave discovered a kindred spirit. Like de Borchgrave, Mariano Fortuny y Madrazo (1871–1949) primarily considered himself a painter but moved easily between a myriad of artistic ventures, working as a photographer as well as a designer of fabric, clothing, theatrical scenery, and stage lighting.

De Borchgrave decided immediately that she wished to capture the totality of Fortuny's oeuvre: "I could not tell his story with just a dress. I wanted to bring the visitor into Fortuny's world, into his palazzo. I needed to create an environment." Drawing on photographs of Fortuny's home, workshop, and boutique as well as his dramatic exhibition at the 1911 Exposition des Arts Décoratifs in Paris, she created an immersive environment of ephemeral pastiche: a tent of feather-light lens paper decorated with lanterns, pillows, and latticework screens, all likewise fabricated from paper. The installation was populated with the silhouette forms that Fortuny used to practice draping. In the corner was a figure of the artist himself, characteristically bedecked in a turban and sitting at his drawing table.

All of de Borchgrave's works are intuitive evocations of original costumes, but her designs became even more interpretative with the Fortuny project. Allowing for greater freedom was a commonality of artistic influences: a textile design vocabulary that freely blends Asian, Coptic, North African, and Renaissance motifs; a fascination with classical painting; and a reverence for ancient cultures. Whether re-creating pleated gowns of fine silk, inspired by ancient Greece and designed to skim the body, or luscious velvet capes with patterns derived from antiquity, de Borchgrave translated Fortuny's sensibility through the media of paper and paint. Both artists mastered the reinterpretation of vintage textiles. Both employed the techniques of stenciling and hand-painting to emulate the look of woven fabric. And both firmly believed in honoring the past and acknowledging influences. As Fortuny himself once wrote, "No trick can hide the origins of a piece of work."

FORTUNY

Fortuny tent, 2006–2007
Inspired by photographs of Fortuny's Venice workshop.
Paris boutique, and display at the 1911 Exposition
des Arts Décoratifs, Paris. Installation by Isabelle
de Borchgrave photographed inside Palazzo Fortuny.

Woman's robe, 2006–2007
Inspired by a design by Fortuny

Delphos dress and coat, 2006–2007
Inspired by a design by Fortuny

Delphos dress and jacket, 2006–2007
Based on a ca. 1910–1930 ensemble by
Fortuny in the collection of the Victoria
and Albert Museum, London

Delphos dress and tunic, 2006–2007
Inspired by a Man Ray photograph of a
design by Fortuny

Dress and coat, 2006–2007
Inspired by a photograph of a
design by Fortuny

Based on a ca. 1924 dress designed
by Fortuny

**Delphos dress and Knossos shawl,
2006–2007**

Based on a ca. 1930 ensemble designed
by Fortuny in the collection of the
Museo Fortuny, Venice

De Borchgrave's most extravagant series found inspiration in the grandeur of the Medici dynasty. Over the course of nearly three centuries, the Medici family, once merchants and bankers, grew into one of the most wealthy and powerful forces in Europe. Their native Florence prospered under Medici reign, becoming the cultural center of the Italian Renaissance. The richness of their legacy still resonates in the magnificent Palazzo Pitti, Boboli Gardens, and Galleria degli Uffizi. The latter, originally built as offices for the Florentine magistrates, now houses one of the world's most impressive collections of Renaissance art, much of it commissioned by the house of Medici. During the reign of Cosimo I (1519–1574), the family began the tradition of commissioning leading artists—including Frans Pourbus the younger, Agnolo Bronzino, Giovanni Bizzelli, Justus Suttermans, and Cristofano Allori—to paint their formal portraits. Political tools intended to display their subjects' power, wealth, intelligence, and cultivation, the portraits show the Medici in their richest finery, emphasizing their access to sumptuous woven textiles and other luxury goods. Indeed, much of the Medici fortune came from bankrolling velvet mills and the silk manufacturers' guild, one of the most influential trade groups of the Renaissance.

When de Borchgrave visited the Uffizi, she yearned for the famous figures to step down out of their gilded frames, "just for the pleasure of walking around them, observing them." With the Medici collection she did just that, reviving the glamour of the Renaissance court. Fashions that have not survived outside of painted depictions took three-dimensional form, their elaborate velvets, needlework lace, ropes of pearls, and intricate coiffures transformed into paper sculpture.

It is telling that de Borchgrave's favorite Medici piece is the dress of Eleanora of Toledo as painted by Bronzino. She was attracted to Eleanora's rich adornment of pearls and gold chains, pointing out that sixteenth-century Italian goldsmiths were unrivaled at their craft. Though de Borchgrave admits that she is no art historian, "I learned in my own way to decipher the story behind the story. I discovered that all the jewelry created by Fulco di Verdura for Chanel in the 1930s was inspired by the dress in the Bronzino portrait!"

the MEDICI

Pallas, 2006
Inspired by the ca. 1482 painting *Pallas and the Centaur* by Sandro Botticelli in the collection of the Galleria degli Uffizi, Florence

Flora, 2006

Inspired by the ca. 1482 painting *Spring* by Sandro Botticelli in the collection of the Galleria degli Uffizi, Florence

Eleanora of Toledo, 2006

Inspired by a ca. 1545 portrait of Eleanora and her son Giovanni de' Medici by Agnolo
Bronzino in the collection of the Galleria degli Uffizi, Florence

Bianca ("Bia") de' Medici, 2006

Inspired by a ca. 1542 portrait by Agnolo Bronzino in the collection of the
Galleria degli Uffizi, Florence

72]

Maria de' Medici, 2006

Inspired by a ca. 1555 portrait by
Alessandro Allori in the collection
of the Kunsthistorisches Museum,
Vienna

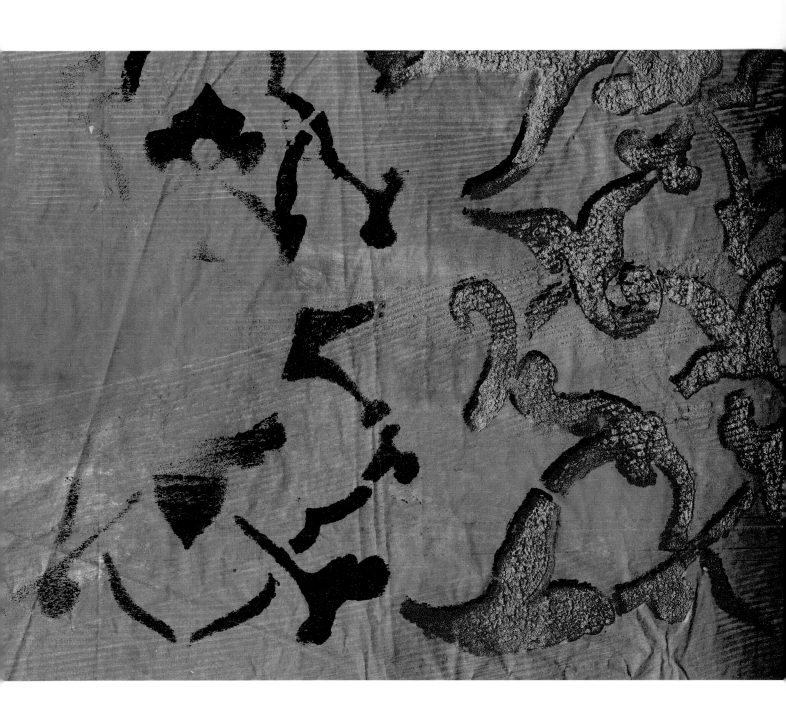

Joanna of Austria, 2006
Inspired by a ca. 1586 portrait of Joanna and her son, Filippo de' Medici, by Giovanni Bizzelli
in the collection of the Galleria degli Uffizi, Florence

Isabella de' Medici, 2006
Inspired by a ca. 1565 portrait attributed to Alessandro Allori in the collection
of the Palazzo Pitti, Florence

Marie de' Medici, 2006

Inspired by a 1595 portrait by Pietro Facchetti in the collection of the
Palazzo Lancellotti, Rome

During a visit to San Francisco's Legion of Honor museum in the summer of 2010, de Borchgrave was captivated by the portrait of a woman in Neapolitan peasant costume by Italian Baroque painter Massimo Stanzione (1585–1656). Whereas de Borchgrave's earlier series were based on depictions of identifiable historical figures or iconic fashion designs, her most recent work homes in on the very ambiguity of her source painting: neither the identity of Stanzione's subject nor the precise meaning of his imagery is known.

It is little wonder that de Borchgrave was fascinated by the young woman's ornate costume. She wears not one but two stiff, tightly fit bodices, elaborately decorated with rows of blue ribbon, embellished with silver threads and buttons, against a crimson ground. Resting upon her shoulders is a scalloped lace collar; more lace trims her inner bodice and linen bonnet. Such an extensive use of lace on a peasant costume is surprising, as seventeenth-century sumptuary laws restricted the wearing of lace to the higher classes. A pink sash binds her red damask apron, beneath which appears a full skirt decorated with fancy ribbons bearing a gold foliate scroll pattern and edged with blue silk floss. She holds in her left hand a rooster. Theories abound regarding the subject of this painting. Is she a provincial woman overdressed in festival garb or a young noblewoman in fanciful peasant costume? Or is the portrait an allegory, the rooster a symbol of jealousy and betrayal?

De Borchgrave's re-creation does not attempt to answer this riddle. She painstakingly attends to every detail, thereby highlighting the painting's most subtle nuances. Every ribbon on the bodice and skirt is an individual strip of paper, meticulously painted, stenciled, and ruffled. The lace collar displays the artist's characteristic handling of intricately cut latticework. And although Stanzione's painting does not show the woman's skirt in its entirety, de Borchgrave has imagined it as an excess of gathered fabric. Tellingly, she has lavished as much attention on the rooster as on the figure's dress, individually crafting each hand-painted feather. The overall effect serves only to emphasize the mysterious tension of Stanzione's portrait.

neapolitan WOMAN

Massimo Stanzione. *Woman in Neapolitan Costume*, ca. 1635.
Oil on canvas. 46¾ × 38¼ in. (118.7 × 97.2 cm). Fine Arts Museums
of San Francisco, 1997.32.

Neapolitan woman, 2010
Inspired by a ca. 1635 portrait by Massimo Stanzione in the
collection of the Fine Arts Museums of San Francisco

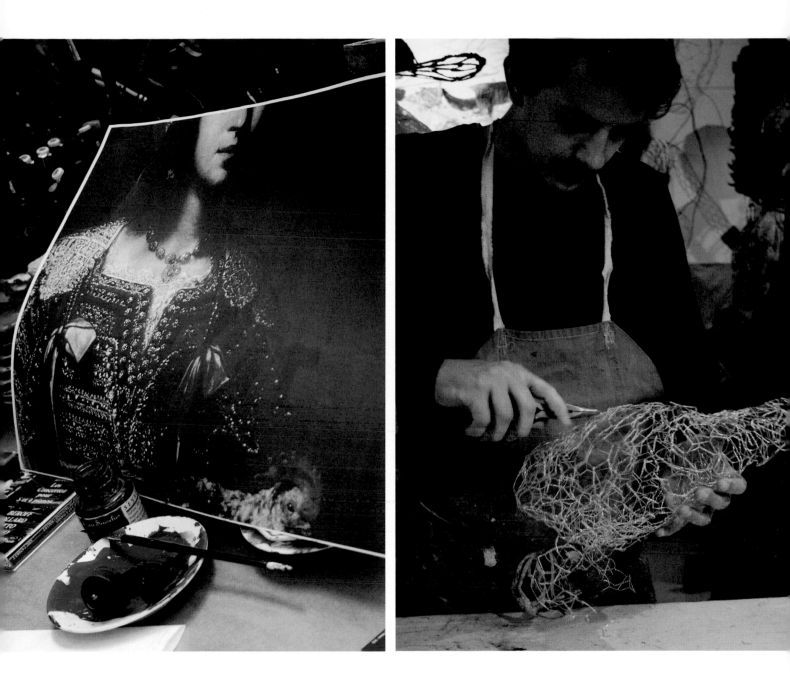

Catalogue of the Exhibition

The following list documents the primary works by Isabelle de Borchgrave featured in the presentation at the Legion of Honor, San Francisco. The exhibition also includes a selection of shoes, purses, and other accessories that complement the objects on display. All works are from the collection of the artist and are made of mixed media, primarily acrylic, ink, metallic powder, and adhesive on paper mounted on wire armatures or mannequins. Notes on de Borchgrave's historical sources are provided whenever available (a work "based on" a source re-creates an actual costume in a museum or private collection; one "inspired by" is a pastiche that borrows from a work of art or an original garment).

White Dresses

"Bar" suit, 2000 (page 4)
Inspired by spring–summer 1947 New Look suits designed by Christian Dior (French, 1905–1957) in the collections of the Costume Institute, the Metropolitan Museum of Art, New York; and the Victoria and Albert Museum, London
76¾ × 26¾ × 31½ in. (195 × 68 × 80 cm)

Court dress, 2000
Inspired by eighteenth-century court dresses with wide panniers
76¾ × 26¾ × 63⅜ in. (195 × 68 × 161 cm)

Day dress, 2000 (page 5)
Based on a ca. 1900 dress designed by Callot Soeurs (French, active 1895–1937) in the collection of the Musée Galliera—Musée de la Mode de la Ville de Paris
76¾ × 26¾ × 31½ in. (195 × 68 × 80 cm)

Evening dress, 2000
Based on a ca. 1866 dress in the collection of the Kyoto Costume Institute
76¾ × 26¾ × 31½ in. (195 × 68 × 80 cm)

Evening dress, 2000
Inspired by a dress depicted in a late-nineteenth-century engraving in *Harper's Bazaar*
76¾ × 26¾ × 33½ in. (195 × 68 × 85 cm)

Evening dress, 2000 (pages 1–3)
Based on a ca. 1903 dress designed by Jacques Antoine Doucet (French, 1853–1929) in the
collection of the Kyoto Costume Institute
76¾ × 26¾ × 33½ in. (195 × 68 × 85 cm)

Evening dress, 2000 (pages 44–45)
Based on a ca. 1924 dress designed by Coco Chanel (French, 1883–1971) in the collection of
the Victoria and Albert Museum, London
76¾ × 26¾ × 31½ in. (195 × 68 × 80 cm)

Evening gown, 2000
Based on a ca. 1806 gown in the collection of the Musée Galliera—Musée de la Mode de la
Ville de Paris
76¾ × 26¾ × 31½ in. (195 × 68 × 80 cm)

Peplos dress, 2006–2007 (page 59)
Based on a ca. 1924 dress designed by Mariano Fortuny y Madrazo (Spanish, active Italy,
1871–1949)
67¾ × 17⅜ × 16⅝ in. (172 × 44 × 42 cm)

Papiers à la Mode

Gown (robe à l'anglaise), 1994
Based on a ca. 1770 gown of hand-painted Chinese export silk in the collection of the
Costume Institute, the Metropolitan Museum of Art, New York
59⅛ × 39⅜ × 31½ in. (150 × 100 × 80 cm)

Pierrot jacket and petticoat, 1994
Based on a ca. 1790 ensemble in the collection of the Kyoto Costume Institute
59⅛ × 39⅜ × 31½ in. (150 × 100 × 80 cm)

Worth evening gown and shoe, 1994 (pages 36–37)
Based on an 1898 dress designed by Charles Frederick Worth (English, active France,
1825–1895) in the collection of the Costume Institute, the Metropolitan Museum of Art,
New York
Dress: 59⅛ × 27⅝ × 59⅛ in. (150 × 70 × 150 cm); shoe: 3⅞ × 8⅝ × 2⅜ in. (10 × 22 × 6 cm)

Gown (robe à la polonaise), 1994–1998
Based on a ca. 1780 gown in the collection of the Kyoto Costume Institute
59⅛ × 39⅜ × 31½ in. (150 × 100 × 80 cm)

Men's formal waistcoat, 1994–1998
Inspired by mid-eighteenth-century waistcoats
65⅜ × 20⅛ × 20⅛ in. (166 × 51 × 51 cm)

Men's formal waistcoat, 1994–1998
Inspired by mid-eighteenth-century waistcoats
65⅜ × 20½ × 16⅛ in. (166 × 52 × 41 cm)

Men's formal waistcoats, 1994–1998
Inspired by mid-eighteenth-century embroidered waistcoats
Five waistcoats, each: 37 × 20⅛ in. (94 × 51 cm)

Sack-back gown (robe à la française), 1994–1998
Based on a ca. 1765 gown in the collection of the Kyoto Costume Institute
59⅛ × 39⅜ × 39¼ in. (150 × 100 × 100 cm)

Paul Poiret evening ensemble and shoe, 1997 (pages 42–43)
Inspired by ca. 1912 ensembles designed by Paul Poiret (French, 1879–1944) in the
    collections of the Costume Institute, the Metropolitan Museum of Art, New York;
    and the Museum of the City of New York
Dress: 53⅝ × 43⅜ × 76¾ in. (136 × 110 × 195 cm); shoe: 6¼ × 9 × 3⅛ in. (16 × 23 × 8 cm)

Round gown, 1997
Based on a ca. 1795 dress in the collection of the Kyoto Costume Institute
59⅛ × 31½ × 51¼ in. (150 × 80 × 130 cm)

American day suit and hat, 1998 (pages 40–41)
Based on a ca. 1900 ensemble in the collection of the Museum at FIT, New York
Dress: 59⅛ × 35¾ × 35¾ in. (150 × 90 × 90 cm); hat: 2 × 13¾ × 12⅝ in. (5 × 35 × 32 cm)

English sporting dress and boater hat, 1998 (pages 38–39)
Based on a ca. 1870 ensemble in the collection of the Victoria and Albert Museum, London
Dress: 66⅝ × 27⅝ × 37 in. (169 × 70 × 94 cm); hat: 3¾ × 12⅝ × 12¼ in. (9.5 × 32 × 31 cm)

Gown (robe à l'anglaise) and shoes, 1998–1999
Based on a ca. 1780 gown of Indian export fabric in the collection of Martin Kamer, London
Dress: 59⅛ × 31½ × 31½ in. (150 × 80 × 80 cm); two shoes, each: 4¾ × 8⅝ × 3⅛ in.
    (12 × 22 × 8 cm)

Elizabeth I court dress, 2001 (pages 30–31)
Inspired by a ca. 1599 portrait by the studio of Nicholas Hilliard (English, ca. 1547–1619) at
    Hardwick Hall, Derbyshire
65 × 37½ × 37½ in. (165 × 95 × 95 cm)

Empress Eugénie evening dress and shoe, 2001 (page 35)
Inspired by the 1856 painting *Madame Moitessier* by Jean-Auguste-Dominique Ingres
    (French, 1780–1867) in the collection of the National Gallery, London
Dress: 65 × 33½ × 33½ in. (165 × 85 × 85 cm); shoe: 2 × 7⅞ × 2¾ in. (5 × 20 × 7 cm)

Madame de Pompadour court dress and shoe, 2001 (pages 32–33)
Inspired by a ca. 1755 portrait by Maurice-Quentin de la Tour (French, 1704–1788) in the
    collection of the Musée du Louvre, Paris, and shoes in the collection of the Costume
    Institute, the Metropolitan Museum of Art, New York
Dress: 65 × 33½ × 25⅝ in. (165 × 85 × 65 cm); shoe: 3⅛ × 8¼ × 3½ in. (8 × 21 × 9 cm)

Margaret Layton evening jacket, 2001 (page 19)
Inspired by a ca. 1610 jacket and a portrait by Marcus Geeraerts the younger (Flemish,
    1561–1635) in the collection of the Victoria and Albert Museum, London
74 × 45⅜ × 29⅝ in. (188 × 115 × 75 cm)

Marie-Antoinette gown , 2001 (page 34)
Inspired by a ca. 1776 engraving in the collection of the Musée du Louvre, Paris
59⅛ × 47¼ × 19¾ in. (150 × 120 × 50 cm)

Men's formal waistcoat, 2001
Inspired by mid-eighteenth-century embroidered waistcoats
65⅜ × 20½ × 16½ in. (166 × 52 × 42 cm)

Fortuny   *All works in this series are inspired by the work of Mariano Fortuny y Madrazo*
(Spanish, active Italy, 1871–1949).

Day ensemble, 2006–2007 (page 50)
Inspired by a ca. 1905 photograph by Fortuny
66⅛ × 22½ × 22 in. (168 × 57 × 56 cm)

Delphos dress, 2006–2007
66⅛ × 19¾ × 19¾ in. (168 × 50 × 50 cm)

Delphos dress and coat, 2006–2007
63 × 17 × 16⅝ in. (160 × 43 × 42 cm)

Delphos dress and coat, 2006–2007 (page 53)
66⅛ × 19¾ × 19¾ in. (168 × 50 × 50 cm)

Delphos dress and jacket, 2006–2007 (page 54)
Based on a ca. 1910–1930 ensemble in the collection of the Victoria and Albert
    Museum, London
66⅝ × 17¾ × 17 in. (169 × 45 × 43 cm)

Delphos dress and jacket, 2006–2007
66⅛ × 21¾ × 17¾ in. (168 × 55 × 45 cm)

Delphos dress and Knossos shawl, 2006–2007 (pages 46, 60–61)
Based on a ca. 1930 ensemble in the collection of the Museo Fortuny, Venice
67¾ × 18½ × 17¾ in. (172 × 47 × 45 cm)

Delphos dress and tunic, 2006–2007 (pages 8–9, 55)
Inspired by a Man Ray photograph of a design by Fortuny
65 × 18½ × 11⅜ in. (165 × 47 × 29 cm)

Delphos dress and tunic, 2006–2007
Inspired by a photograph of a design by Fortuny
66⅛ × 21⅝ × 17¾ in. (168 × 55 × 45 cm)

Dress, 2006–2007
Inspired by a ca. 1920 design in an autochrome photograph by Fortuny
66⅝ × 18½ × 11⁷⁄₁₆ in. (169 × 47 × 29 cm)

Dress and coat, 2006–2007 (pages 56–58)
Inspired by a photograph of a design by Fortuny
62¼ × 28¾ × 22⅞ in. (158 × 73 × 58 cm)

Fortuny closet, 2006–2007
Installation containing nine dresses inspired by ca. 1910–1930 designs
Dimensions variable

Fortuny tent, 2006–2007 (pages 48–49)
Inspired by photographs of Fortuny's Venice workshop, Paris boutique, and display
    at the 1911 Exposition des Arts Décoratifs, Paris
177$\frac{1}{8}$ × 196$\frac{7}{8}$ × 196$\frac{7}{8}$ in. (450 × 500 × 500 cm)

Peplos dress and coat, 2006–2007
66$\frac{1}{8}$ × 19$\frac{3}{4}$ × 19$\frac{3}{4}$ in. (168 × 50 × 50 cm)

Theater costume, 2006–2007
Inspired by a design in an autochrome photograph by Fortuny
Dress: 66$\frac{1}{8}$ × 31$\frac{1}{2}$ × 19$\frac{3}{4}$ in. (168 × 95 × 50 cm); coat: 61$\frac{1}{8}$ × 53$\frac{1}{4}$ × 23$\frac{5}{8}$ in.
    (155 × 135 × 60 cm)

Woman's robe, 2006–2007 (page 51)
66$\frac{1}{8}$ × 29$\frac{5}{8}$ × 27$\frac{5}{8}$ in. (168 × 75 × 70 cm)

The Medici

Anna de' Medici (1616–1676), 2006
Inspired by a 1622 portrait by Justus Suttermans (Flemish, active Italy, 1597–1681) in the
    collection of the Galleria degli Uffizi, Florence
49$\frac{5}{8}$ × 26$\frac{3}{8}$ × 31$\frac{1}{8}$ in. (126 × 67 × 79 cm)

Anna Maria Luisa de' Medici (1667–1743), 2006
Inspired by a 1708 portrait of Anna Maria Luisa and her husband, Johann Wilhelm, by Jan
    Frans Douven (Dutch, 1656–1727) in the collection of the Galleria degli Uffizi, Florence
54$\frac{3}{4}$ × 36$\frac{5}{8}$ × 36$\frac{1}{4}$ in. (139 × 93 × 92 cm)

Bianca ("Bia") de' Medici (ca. 1536–1542), 2006 (pages 72–73)
Inspired by a ca. 1542 portrait by Agnolo Bronzino (Italian, 1503–1572) in the collection of
    the Galleria degli Uffizi, Florence
47$\frac{5}{8}$ × 20$\frac{1}{2}$ × 18$\frac{1}{8}$ in. (121 × 52 × 46 cm)

Catherine de' Medici (1519–1589), 2006
Inspired by a sixteenth-century portrait in the collection of the Palazzo Pitti, Florence
73$\frac{1}{4}$ × 59$\frac{1}{2}$ × 31$\frac{1}{2}$ in. (186 × 151 × 80 cm)

Catherine de' Medici (1593–1629), 2006
Inspired by an early-seventeenth-century portrait of Francesco and Catherine de' Medici by
    Cristofano Allori (Italian, 1577–1621) in the collection of the Palazzo Pitti, Florence
48$\frac{1}{8}$ × 30$\frac{3}{4}$ × 29$\frac{1}{8}$ in. (122 × 78 × 74 cm)

Eleanora of Toledo (1522–1562), 2006 (pages 12, 68–71)
Inspired by a ca. 1545 portrait of Eleanora and her son Giovanni de' Medici by Agnolo
    Bronzino (Italian, 1503–1572) in the collection of the Galleria degli Uffizi, Florence
72$\frac{1}{2}$ × 42$\frac{1}{2}$ × 26$\frac{3}{8}$ in. (184 × 108 × 67 cm)

Flora, 2006 (pages 66–67)

Inspired by the ca. 1482 painting *Spring* by Sandro Botticelli (Italian, 1444/1445–1510)
  in the collection of the Galleria degli Uffizi, Florence

74½ × 26¾ × 25¼ in. (188 × 68 × 64 cm)

Gian Carlo de' Medici (1611–1663), 2006

Inspired by a ca. 1622 portrait attributed to Justus Suttermans (Flemish, active Italy,
  1597–1681) in the collection of the Galleria degli Uffizi, Florence

47⅝ × 20½ × 18⅛ in. (121 × 52 × 46 cm)

Isabella de' Medici (1542–1576), 2006 (pages 8, 78–79)

Inspired by a ca. 1565 portrait attributed to Alessandro Allori (Italian, 1535–1607) in the
  collection of the Palazzo Pitti, Florence

71¾ × 36¼ × 35½ in. (182 × 92 × 90 cm)

Joanna of Austria (1546–1578), 2006 (pages 76–77)

Inspired by a ca. 1586 portrait of Joanna and her son, Filippo de' Medici, by Giovanni Bizzelli
  (Italian, 1556–1612) in the collection of the Galleria degli Uffizi, Florence

76⅞ × 48½ × 40⅝ in. (195 × 123 × 103 cm)

Leopoldo de' Medici (1617–1675), 2006

Inspired by a ca. 1622 portrait by Justus Suttermans (Flemish, active Italy, 1597–1681) in the
  collection of the Galleria degli Uffizi, Florence

51¼ × 35½ × 28¾ in. (130 × 90 × 73 cm)

Maria de' Medici (1540–1557), 2006 (pages 62, 74–75)

Inspired by a ca. 1555 portrait by Alessandro Allori (Italian, 1535–1607) in the collection of
  the Kunsthistorisches Museum, Vienna

72⅞ × 36⅝ × 32¾ in. (185 × 93 × 83 cm)

Maria Maddalena of Austria (1589–1631), 2006

Inspired by a ca. 1623 portrait of Maria Maddalena and her son Ferdinando de' Medici by
  Justus Suttermans (Flemish, active Italy, 1597–1681) in the collection of the Flint Institute
  of Arts, Michigan

72⅞ × 39⅜ × 38⅝ in. (185 × 100 × 98 cm)

Marie de' Medici (1573–1642), 2006 (pages 80–81)

Inspired by a 1595 portrait by Pietro Facchetti (Italian, 1535/1539–1619) in the collection of
  the Palazzo Lancellotti, Rome

72⅛ × 43⅜ × 46½ in. (183 × 110 × 118 cm)

Marie de' Medici (1573–1642), 2006

Inspired by a 1611 portrait by Frans Pourbus the younger (Flemish, 1569–1622) in the
  collection of the Palazzo Pitti, Florence

72⅛ × 53¼ × 26¾ in. (183 × 135 × 68 cm)

Pallas, 2006 (pages 64–65)

Inspired by the ca. 1482 painting *Pallas and the Centaur* by Sandro Botticelli (Italian,
  1444/1445–1510) in the collection of the Galleria degli Uffizi, Florence

74 × 34¼ × 23¼ in. (189 × 87 × 59 cm)

New Work

Anna Caffarelli Minuttiba, 2010

Inspired by a late-seventeenth-century portrait by Jacob-Ferdinand Voet (Flemish, 1639–ca. 1700) in the collection of the Fine Arts Museums of San Francisco

Approx. 74²/₃ × 31¹/₂ × 25⁵/₈ in. (190 × 80 × 65 cm)

Bridesmaid, 2010

Inspired by the 1889 painting *The Russian Bride's Attire* by Konstantin Makovsky (Russian, 1839–1915) in the collection of the Fine Arts Museums of San Francisco

Approx. 74²/₃ × 31¹/₂ × 25⁵/₈ in. (190 × 80 × 65 cm)

Marie Claire de Croy and child, 2010

Inspired by a 1634 portrait by Anthony van Dyck (Flemish, 1599–1641) in the collection of the Fine Arts Museums of San Francisco

Two pieces, approx. 74²/₃ × 31¹/₂ × 25⁵/₈ in. (190 × 80 × 65 cm) and 47⁵/₈ × 20¹/₂ × 18¹/₈ in. (121 × 52 × 46 cm)

Neapolitan woman, 2010 (pages 10, 82, 85–93)

Inspired by a ca. 1635 portrait by Massimo Stanzione (Italian, 1585–1656) in the collection of the Fine Arts Museums of San Francisco

Approx. 74²/₃ × 31¹/₂ × 25⁵/₈ in. (190 × 80 × 65 cm)

Suggested Further Reading

Deschodt, Ann-Marie, and Doretta Davanzo Poli. *Fortuny*. New York: Harry N. Abrams, 2001.

Fortuny. New York: Galleries at the Fashion Institute of Technology; Chicago: Art Institute of Chicago, 1981.

Fortuny: El mago de Venecia. Barcelona: Fundacio Caixa Catalunya, Obra Social, 2010.

Fukai, Akiko, and Tamami Suoh. *Fashion: The Collection of the Kyoto Costume Institute*. Cologne: Taschen, 2002.

Hoeveler, David J. *The Postmodernist Turn: American Thought and Culture in the 1970s*. New York: Twayne Publishers, 1996.

Jensen, Robert, and Patricia Conway. *Ornamentalism: The New Decorativeness in Architecture and Design*. New York: Clarkson N. Potter, 1982.

Judah, Hettie. "Trompe-l'oeil Couture." *The Bulletin*, March 20, 2008.

Koda, Harold, and Andrew Bolton. *Dangerous Liaisons: Fashion and Furniture in the Eighteenth Century*. New York: Metropolitan Museum of Art; New Haven, CT: Yale University Press, 2006.

Un mondo di carta: Isabelle de Borchgrave incontra Mariano Fortuny. Milan: Skira, 2008.

Nash, Stephen A., Lynn Federle Orr, and Marion C. Stewart. *Masterworks of European Painting in the California Palace of the Legion of Honor*. San Francisco: Fine Arts Museums of San Francisco, 1999.

Nuzzi, Cristina. *Fortuny nella Belle Epoque*. Milan: Electa, 1984.

Porter, Jeanne Chenault, and Susan Scott Munshower, eds. *Parthenope's Splendor: Art of the Golden Age in Naples*. Papers in Art History from the Pennsylvania State University 7. University Park, PA: Pennsylvania State University, 1993.

Ribeiro, Aileen. *The Art of Dress: Fashion in England and France, 1750–1820*. New Haven, CT: Yale University Press, 1995.

———. *The Gallery of Fashion*. Princeton, NJ: Princeton University Press, 2000.

Sandler, Irving. *Art of the Postmodern Era: From the Late 1960s to the Early 1990s*. Boulder, CO: Westview Press, 1998.

Starobinski, Jean, et al. *Revolution in Fashion: European Clothing, 1715–1815*. New York: Abbeville Press, 1989.

Stoeltie, Barbara and René. *Paper Illusions: The Art of Isabelle de Borchgrave*. New York: Harry N. Abrams, 2008.

Swartz, Anne, ed. *Pattern and Decoration: An Ideal Vision in American Art, 1975–1985*. New York: Hudson River Museum, 2007.

Zidianakis, Vassilis. *Rrripp!! Paper Fashion*. Athens: ATOPOS Foundation, 2007.

Frontispieces   *All works collection of the artist. See the catalogue of the exhibition (pages 95–101) for additional information.*

Pages 1–3: Evening dress, 2000
Based on a ca. 1903 dress designed by Jacques Antoine Doucet in the collection of the Kyoto Costume Institute

Page 4: "Bar" suit, 2000
Inspired by spring–summer 1947 New Look suits designed by Christian Dior in the collections of the Costume Institute, the Metropolitan Museum of Art, New York; and the Victoria and Albert Museum, London

Page 5: Day dress, 2000
Based on a ca. 1900 dress designed by Callot Soeurs in the collection of the Musée Galliera—Musée de la Mode de la Ville de Paris

Pages 6–7: Page from one of Isabelle de Borchgrave's sketchbooks showing photographs of various white dresses, ca. 2000

Page 8: Isabella de' Medici (detail), 2006
Inspired by a ca. 1565 portrait attributed to Alessandro Allori in the collection of the Palazzo Pitti, Florence

Pages 8–9: Delphos dress and tunic (detail), 2006–2007
Inspired by a Man Ray photograph of a design by Mariano Fortuny y Madrazo

Pages 10 and 82: Neapolitan woman (detail), 2010
Inspired by a ca. 1635 portrait by Massimo Stanzione in the collection of the Fine Arts Museums of San Francisco

Page 28: Worth evening gown (detail), 1994
Based on an 1898 dress designed by Charles Frederick Worth in the collection of the Costume Institute, the Metropolitan Museum of Art, New York

Page 46: Delphos dress and Knossos shawl (detail), 2006–2007
Based on a ca. 1930 ensemble designed by Mariano Fortuny y Madrazo in the collection of the Museo Fortuny, Venice

Page 62: Maria de' Medici (detail), 2006
Inspired by a ca. 1555 portrait by Alessandro Allori in the collection of the Kunsthistorisches Museum, Vienna

Photography Credits   *Unless otherwise indicated below, images are provided courtesy Créations Isabelle de Borchgrave and reproduced by permission of the artist.*

Pages 1, 2, 3, 4, 5, 6–7, 8, 19 (left), 28, 30, 31, 32, 33 (top), 34, 35, 36 (top), 37, 38, 39, 40, 41, 42, 44, 45, 62, 64, 67, 69, 72, 73, 74, 75, 76, 78, 79, 80, 81: Andreas von Einsiedel; 8–9, 46, 50, 55, 56, 56–57, 59, 60, 61: Jean-Pierre Gabriel; 10, 51, 52–53, 66, 70–71, 82, 85, 90, 91, 92, 93: René Stoeltie; 16, 33 (bottom), 36 (bottom), 86, 87, 88, 89, 95, 97, 99, 101: Pauline de Borchgrave; 19 (right), 23, 84: Joseph McDonald, © Fine Arts Museums of San Francisco; 22: © National Gallery, London/Art Resource, NY; 24: courtesy DC Moore Gallery, New York; 48–49: Charles-Édouard Mosneron Dupin, installation by Isabelle de Borchgrave photographed inside Palazzo Fortuny; 54, 58: Philippe Leclercq.

pulp FASHION

Published by the Fine Arts Museums of San Francisco and DelMonico Books, an imprint of Prestel Publishing, on the occasion of the exhibition *Pulp Fashion: The Art of Isabelle de Borchgrave*, on view at the Legion of Honor from February 5 through June 5, 2011.

Pulp Fashion: The Art of Isabelle de Borchgrave is organized by the Fine Arts Museums of San Francisco and sponsored by Lonna Wais. Additional support is provided by Elizabeth W. Vobach. Collection Connections is made possible by The Annenberg Foundation.

The catalogue is supported in part by a grant from Friends of Fiber Art International.

Photography credits appear on page 103.

Library of Congress Cataloging-in-Publication Data

D'Alessandro, Jill.
  Pulp fashion : the art of Isabelle de Borchgrave / Jill D'Alessandro.
    p. cm.
    Published on the occasion of an exhibition held at the Legion of Honor, San Francisco, Feb. 5–June 5, 2011.
    ISBN 978-3-7913-5105-6 (hardcover)
    1. Paper work—Exhibitions. 2. Paper garments—Exhibitions. 3. De Borchgrave, Isabelle—Exhibitions. I. De Borchgrave, Isabelle. II. Legion of Honor (San Francisco, Calif.). III. Title. IV. Title: Art of Isabelle de Borchgrave.
  GT511.D35 2010
  746.9'2074794'61—dc22   2010033816

Fine Arts Museums of San Francisco
Golden Gate Park
50 Hagiwara Tea Garden Drive
San Francisco, CA 94118-4502

Karen A. Levine, Director of Publications

Prestel, a member of Verlagsgruppe Random House GmbH

Prestel Verlag
Königinstrasse 9
80539 Munich
Germany
Tel: 49 89 24 29 08 300
Fax: 49 89 24 29 08 335
www.prestel.de

Prestel Publishing Ltd.
4 Bloomsbury Place
London WC1A 2QA
United Kingdom
Tel: 44 20 7323 5004
Fax: 44 20 7636 8004

Prestel Publishing
900 Broadway, Suite 603
New York, NY 10003
United States
Tel: 212 995 2720
Fax: 212 995 2733
E-mail: sales@prestel-usa.com
www.prestel.com

Edited by Karen A. Levine
Proofread by Danica Hodge and Carrie Wicks
Designed and typeset by Susan E. Kelly
Set in Filosofia and Knockout
Color management by iocolor, Seattle
Produced by Marquand Books, Inc., Seattle
    www.marquand.com
Printed and bound in China by C&C Offset Printing Co., Ltd.